CONTENTMENT FOUND IN CONFINEMENT

PANDEMIC POETRY AND PROSE

STEPHANIE OLIVIA BELL

To order additional copies of this book, contact:
Xlibris
844-714-8691
www.Xlibris.com
Orders@Xlibris.com

ISBN: Softcover   978-1-6698-5796-9
           EBook   978-1-6698-5795-2

Print information available on the last page

Rev. date: 11/30/2022

A Note from the author:

If you have any comments about this booklet, I would love to hear from you. Thank you.

Send me your comments to:
stephaniebelleagle@me.com

I have always turned to paper and pen when excited, in wonder or distressed. I have found that writing down the obtrusive thoughts frees the mind.

I have chosen poetry as the venue. Hopefully, you too can relate. I hope that you may glean some insight into yourself and find peace, joy and some wisdom.

I may add that some of the poetry is obvious. Others need to be read more than once. As in a painting, the observer gets out of it what relates to her. So too in poetry. You may read a poem and feel something entirely different from why I wrote it.

That is just fine. My purpose was personal. Your purpose could be that the poem stimulates a remembrance of a time in your life that can be relived. Enjoy.

Stephanie Olivia Bell

The Stay Vacation

Are you enjoying your "Stay Vacation?" Yes!
Today, April 5th, 2020
A window washer shower,
Palm Sunday, and
John's 80th Birthday,

We went to ZOOM Church,
Admiring our lake and mountain views
From John's office computer.
A new experience on Palm Sunday.

Now the service is over.
The shower is gaining momentum.
A raven just flew by.
The wind is moving the trees.

Another week begins
on our "Stay Vacation."

WASH YOUR HANDS,
DON'T TOUCH YOUR FACE

Some call it prison
Incarcerated.
Unable to leave.

Our home is a blessing.
Three stories in which to wander.
Views from every level.

Views you say? Oh yes.
The moon, the stars, the sun
landing on our bed morning and night.

Outside, the quail, birds and swans;
Rosemary, fruit trees, roses,
Puffy clouds, mountains, a lake and wind.

What to do with all this time?
Use the Jacuzzi, the dry sauna,
Walk the deck and watch the changing scene.

Go back in time,
Back through boxes, boxes and more boxes.
I seemed to have saved everything.

Everything from
Camp, grammar school, high school, college,
Real Estate, Rotary, Toastmasters.
Saved pictures, letters, trips,
Evoking
Memory after memory of happiness.
I just might not want this to end. After all, food can be delivered.
And how I know how to Zoom!

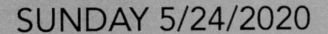

SUNDAY 5/24/2020

I awoke to
the baking banana bread
wafting through the vents.

My husband,
the baker
is practicing his art.

He also
bakes bagels
and makes liver pate.

We used to fight
for kitchen rights.
Now we share.

He will always
be
the BBQ King.

OBSERVATIONS

You know the huge black Raven?
The one that flies by on a regular basis?
Well, this evening about 5:10pm,
after having a drink or two of water,
he took a bath in the deep end of the infinity pool.
He landed on the shallow edge,
strutted along until he came to the deep end.

For at least 8 minutes in the shade of the pool,
he dunked his head again, again and again.
Believe me, I thought he was going
to take a swim, so immersed was he.
As a thank you he turned around,
and pooped in the pool,
prior to flying off to dry his feathers in the air currant.

You are welcome Raven.
Come back anytime

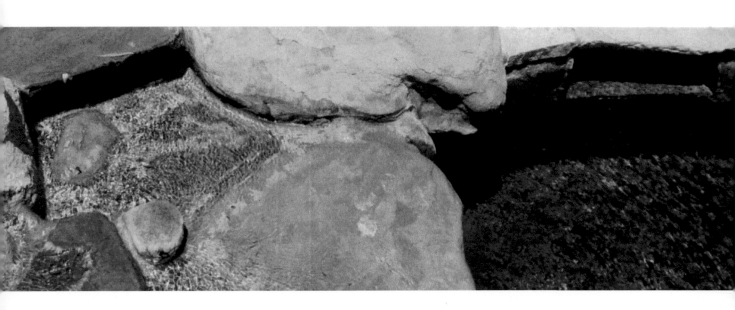

MY FORTUNE

The white round moon
nestled in the cloudless blue sky.
And it is only late afternoon.

Where Mr. moon will you be this evening?
Shinning on my bed again along with the stars?
I surely hope so.

An airline plane bound for LAX
just skimmed underneath the moon
leaving it alone again in the blue sky.

The lake is riddled with boats.
Party boats, canoes, paddle boats
gliding through the still calm waters.

I have come to the realization,
being housebound is not so bad.
When fortune allows all that I can see.

EARLY MORNING

The music of silence.
Butterflies floating by
Casting a soft shadow
with the help of the rising sun.

Too early for the chirping birds,
the morning doves' coo,
the watchful father quail
minding his flock.

Silence. Quiet.
Oh joy, not a barking dog,
not a maintenance truck
nor a gardeners' leafy blower.

Soon, the sun will rise.
The trees will move in gentle winds.
Gone the music of silence.
Let the day begin.

OPEN YOUR EYES

Life is a journey.
God knows the path.
Detours come for a reason.

Revel in them.
Placed in your path
for a reason.

How do you react?
With anger, upset or
learn from the experience.

Remember,
God knows your path.
He will not lead you astray.

There is something
to be gained from the detour.
Open your eyes.

LIVING ON THE EDGE

The father quail,
The dove,
The raven.

All birds in residence.
We have an infinity edge
to the swimming pool.

In alternate hours of the day,
one or the other is
sitting, drinking, bathing on the edge.

In this time of confinement,
are you living on the edge
or taking it in stride?

Think about it.
Pretty brave of the birds
to be living on the edge.

A full pool of water.
Only the infinity edge
To separate from the overflow trough.

re you hovering between
the drop off of the edge or
gathering strength to lift off?

Life's choices

FARMER JOHN

I am blessed with the bounty of our land.
Thanks be to God and John.
Early Girl tomatoes, watermelons, figs,
grapes, rosemary, flowers in abundance.
Thanks to my husband.

Hummingbirds, Wrens, Blackbirds,
Doves, the several families of Quail,
all because of John who feeds and
refills their food source and
the lovely weather which adds to the joy.

TWILIGHT

Evening shade has covered
the patio deck and feeding grounds.
I have my 5:30 ritual and view,
Martini and pistachio nuts.

Watching the birds feeding
Is soul nurturing.
Some bathing on the infinity
edge of the pool.

Absolute stillness.
Noise abated, windless sky.
No TV, no radio, no traffic.
Peace at the last.

MY RENTAL PROPERTY

Can you walk
on top of a Rosemary thatch?
"Well, yes I can" said the Quail.

And so it went.
I gave no permission
to the relocating families.

They have moved in
lock, stock and barrel.
Should I charge them rent?

Three families raising their young.
Need more room, in the annex now.
Time to charge them rent.

They have the run of the land.
Drink from the pool,
eat bird feeder fallings.

What do I get in return?
Their beautiful sounds and
watching their families grow.

I have decided not to charge rent.
My pleasure is to have them as guests.
Walk on top or under the Rosemary anytime.

Printed in the United States
by Baker & Taylor Publisher Services